Congratulations on making the decision to keep track of your scores, goals, thoughts, and dreams.

Whether you are just beginning to compete or you've been competing for several years, keeping a journal is a great way to set goals and preserve memories.

Years from now this journal may be picked up and the reader will be brought back in time.

Maybe the goals will be reached or maybe they will be changed, but at the very least the gymnast using this journal will have preserved gymnastics moments and memories.

My Scores, My Goals, My Dreams... My Journal

Date of Meet _____

Name of Meet _____

Location of Meet _____

Level Competing Today _____

My Teammates Today _____

_____

My Coach Today _____

How am I going to relax today? _____

_____

Am I ready to focus? _____

_____

Main Goal for Meet _____

_____

_____

Event & Score Goals for Today _____

Beam _____

Bars _____

Floor _____

Vault _____

All Around _____

Scores Today

Vault	Bars	Beam	Floor	AA
8.475	9.000	8.950	9.150	

Did I meet my score goals? _____

What mistakes did I make today? _____

_____

Will I do anything differently next meet? _____

_____

Main Goal for Next Meet

_____

_____

Event & Score Goals for Next Meet

Beam _____

Bars _____

Floor _____

Vault _____

All Around _____

One Month Goals

_____

_____

_____

End of Season Goals

_____

_____

One Year Goals

_____

_____

_____

_____

My Dreams

_____

_____

_____

_____

My Thoughts

_____

_____

_____

My Scores, My Goals, My Dreams... My Journal

My Scores, My Goals, My Dreams… My Journal

My Scores, My Goals, My Dreams... My Journal

Date of Meet _____

Name of Meet _____

Location of Meet _____

Level Competing Today _____

My Teammates Today _____

_____

_____

My Coach Today _____

How am I going to relax today? _____

_____

Am I ready to focus? _____

_____

Main Goal for Meet _____

_____

_____

_____

Event & Score Goals for Today

Beam _____

Bars _____

Floor _____

Vault _____

All Around _____

Scores Today

Vault	Bars	Beam	Floor	AA

Did I meet my score goals? _____

What mistakes did I make today? _____

_____

Will I do anything differently next meet? _____

_____

My Scores, My Goals, My Dreams... My Journal

<u>Main Goal for Next Meet</u>
_____
_____

<u>Event & Score Goals for Next Meet</u>
Beam _____
Bars _____
Floor _____
Vault _____
All Around _____

<u>One Month Goals</u>
_____
_____
_____

<u>End of Season Goals</u>
_____
_____

<u>One Year Goals</u>
_____
_____
_____
_____

<u>My Dreams</u>
_____
_____
_____
_____

<u>My Thoughts</u>
_____
_____
_____

My Scores, My Goals, My Dreams... My Journal

My Scores, My Goals, My Dreams… My Journal

Date of Meet

Name of Meet

Location of Meet

Level Competing Today

My Teammates Today

My Coach Today

How am I going to relax today?

Am I ready to focus?

Main Goal for Meet

Event & Score Goals for Today

Beam

Bars

Floor

Vault

All Around

Scores Today

Vault	Bars	Beam	Floor	AA

Did I meet my score goals?

What mistakes did I make today?

Will I do anything differently next meet?

Main Goal for Next Meet
_____
_____

Event & Score Goals for Next Meet
Beam _____
Bars _____
Floor _____
Vault _____
All Around _____

One Month Goals
_____
_____
_____

End of Season Goals
_____
_____

One Year Goals
_____
_____
_____
_____

My Dreams
_____
_____
_____
_____

My Thoughts
_____
_____
_____

My Scores, My Goals, My Dreams... My Journal

© 2005 Goeller

My Scores, My Goals, My Dreams… My Journal

Date of Meet _____

Name of Meet _____

Location of Meet _____

Level Competing Today _____

My Teammates Today _____

_____

My Coach Today _____

How am I going to relax today? _____

_____

Am I ready to focus? _____

_____

Main Goal for Meet _____

_____

_____

Event & Score Goals for Today

Beam _____

Bars _____

Floor _____

Vault _____

All Around _____

Scores Today

Vault	Bars	Beam	Floor	AA

Did I meet my score goals? _____

What mistakes did I make today? _____

Will I do anything differently next meet? _____

_____

Main Goal for Next Meet

_____

_____

Event & Score Goals for Next Meet
Beam _____
Bars _____
Floor _____
Vault _____
All Around _____

One Month Goals

_____

_____

End of Season Goals

_____

One Year Goals

_____

_____

_____

My Dreams

_____

_____

_____

My Thoughts

_____

_____

My Scores, My Goals, My Dreams... My Journal

My Scores, My Goals, My Dreams... My Journal

Date of Meet

Name of Meet

Location of Meet

Level Competing Today

My Teammates Today

My Coach Today

How am I going to relax today?

Am I ready to focus?

Main Goal for Meet

Event & Score Goals for Today

Beam

Bars

Floor

Vault

All Around

Scores Today

Vault	Bars	Beam	Floor	AA

Did I meet my score goals?

What mistakes did I make today?

Will I do anything differently next meet?

Main Goal for Next Meet

_____
_____

Event & Score Goals for Next Meet

Beam _____
Bars _____
Floor _____
Vault _____
All Around _____

One Month Goals

_____
_____
_____

End of Season Goals

_____
_____

One Year Goals

_____
_____
_____
_____

My Dreams

_____
_____
_____
_____

My Thoughts

_____
_____
_____

My Scores, My Goals, My Dreams… My Journal

My Scores, My Goals, My Dreams... My Journal

Date of Meet _____

Name of Meet _____

Location of Meet _____

Level Competing Today _____

My Teammates Today _____

_____

_____

My Coach Today _____

How am I going to relax today? _____

_____

Am I ready to focus? _____

_____

Main Goal for Meet _____

_____

_____

Event & Score Goals for Today _____

Beam _____

Bars _____

Floor _____

Vault _____

All Around _____

Scores Today _____

Vault	Bars	Beam	Floor	AA

Did I meet my score goals? _____

What mistakes did I make today? _____

_____

Will I do anything differently next meet? __

_____

Main Goal for Next Meet
_____
_____

Event & Score Goals for Next Meet
Beam _____
Bars _____
Floor _____
Vault _____
All Around _____

One Month Goals
_____
_____
_____

End of Season Goals
_____
_____

One Year Goals
_____
_____
_____
_____

My Dreams
_____
_____
_____
_____

My Thoughts
_____
_____
_____

My Scores, My Goals, My Dreams... My Journal

My Scores, My Goals, My Dreams... My Journal

Date of Meet _____

Name of Meet _____

Location of Meet _____

Level Competing Today _____

My Teammates Today _____

_____

_____

My Coach Today _____

How am I going to relax today? _____

_____

Am I ready to focus? _____

_____

Main Goal for Meet _____

_____

_____

Event & Score Goals for Today _____

Beam _____

Bars _____

Floor _____

Vault _____

All Around _____

Scores Today _____

Vault	Bars	Beam	Floor	AA

Did I meet my score goals? _____

What mistakes did I make today? _____

_____

Will I do anything differently next meet? _____

_____

Main Goal for Next Meet

_____

_____

Event & Score Goals for Next Meet

Beam _____

Bars _____

Floor _____

Vault _____

All Around _____

One Month Goals

_____

_____

_____

End of Season Goals

_____

_____

One Year Goals

_____

_____

_____

_____

My Dreams

_____

_____

_____

_____

My Thoughts

_____

_____

_____

My Scores, My Goals, My Dreams... My Journal

My Scores, My Goals, My Dreams… My Journal

Date of Meet _____

Name of Meet _____

Location of Meet _____

Level Competing Today _____

My Teammates Today _____

_____

_____

My Coach Today _____

How am I going to relax today? _____

_____

Am I ready to focus? _____

_____

Main Goal for Meet _____

_____

_____

Event & Score Goals for Today _____

Beam _____

Bars _____

Floor _____

Vault _____

All Around _____

Scores Today _____

Vault	Bars	Beam	Floor	AA

Did I meet my score goals? _____

What mistakes did I make today? _____

Will I do anything differently next meet? _____

_____

Main Goal for Next Meet

_____

_____

Event & Score Goals for Next Meet

Beam _____

Bars _____

Floor _____

Vault _____

All Around _____

One Month Goals

_____

_____

_____

End of Season Goals

_____

_____

One Year Goals

_____

_____

_____

_____

My Dreams

_____

_____

_____

_____

My Thoughts

_____

_____

_____

My Scores, My Goals, My Dreams... My Journal

My Scores, My Goals, My Dreams... My Journal

Date of Meet _____

Name of Meet _____

Location of Meet _____

Level Competing Today _____

My Teammates Today _____

_____

_____

My Coach Today _____

How am I going to relax today? _____

_____

Am I ready to focus? _____

_____

Main Goal for Meet _____

_____

_____

Event & Score Goals for Today _____

Beam _____

Bars _____

Floor _____

Vault _____

All Around _____

Scores Today _____

Vault_____Bars_____Beam_____Floor_____AA

_____

Did I meet my score goals? _____

What mistakes did I make today? _____

_____

Will I do anything differently next meet? _____

_____

Main Goal for Next Meet

_____

_____

Event & Score Goals for Next Meet

Beam _____

Bars _____

Floor _____

Vault _____

All Around _____

One Month Goals

_____

_____

_____

End of Season Goals

_____

_____

One Year Goals

_____

_____

_____

_____

My Dreams

_____

_____

_____

_____

My Thoughts

_____

_____

_____

My Scores, My Goals, My Dreams... My Journal

_____
_____
_____
_____
_____
_____
_____
_____
_____
_____
_____
_____
_____
_____
_____
_____
_____
_____
_____
_____
_____
_____
_____
_____
_____
_____
_____
_____
_____

© 2005 Goeller

My Scores, My Goals, My Dreams… My Journal

Date of Meet _____

Name of Meet _____

Location of Meet _____

Level Competing Today _____

My Teammates Today _____

_____

_____

My Coach Today _____

How am I going to relax today? _____

_____

Am I ready to focus? _____

_____

Main Goal for Meet _____

_____

_____

Event & Score Goals for Today _____

Beam _____

Bars _____

Floor _____

Vault _____

All Around _____

Scores Today

Vault	Bars	Beam	Floor	AA

Did I meet my score goals? _____

What mistakes did I make today? _____

_____

Will I do anything differently next meet? _____

_____

Main Goal for Next Meet

_____
_____

Event & Score Goals for Next Meet

Beam _____
Bars _____
Floor _____
Vault _____
All Around _____

One Month Goals

_____
_____
_____

End of Season Goals

_____
_____

One Year Goals

_____
_____
_____
_____

My Dreams

_____
_____
_____
_____

My Thoughts

_____
_____
_____

My Scores, My Goals, My Dreams... My Journal

My Scores, My Goals, My Dreams… My Journal

My Scores, My Goals, My Dreams… My Journal

Date of Meet _____

Name of Meet _____

Location of Meet _____

Level Competing Today _____

My Teammates Today _____

_____

My Coach Today _____

How am I going to relax today? _____

_____

Am I ready to focus? _____

_____

Main Goal for Meet _____

_____

_____

Event & Score Goals for Today _____

Beam _____

Bars _____

Floor _____

Vault _____

All Around _____

Scores Today

Vault   Bars   Beam   Floor   AA

_____

Did I meet my score goals? _____

What mistakes did I make today? _____

_____

Will I do anything differently next meet? ____

_____

Main Goal for Next Meet

Event & Score Goals for Next Meet
Beam
Bars
Floor
Vault
All Around

One Month Goals

End of Season Goals

One Year Goals

My Dreams

My Thoughts

My Scores, My Goals, My Dreams... My Journal

My Scores, My Goals, My Dreams… My Journal

Date of Meet _____

Name of Meet _____

Location of Meet _____

Level Competing Today _____

My Teammates Today _____

_____

_____

My Coach Today _____

How am I going to relax today? _____

_____

Am I ready to focus? _____

_____

Main Goal for Meet _____

_____

_____

Event & Score Goals for Today _____

Beam _____

Bars _____

Floor _____

Vault _____

All Around _____

Scores Today _____

Vault	Bars	Beam	Floor	AA

Did I meet my score goals? _____

What mistakes did I make today? _____

_____

Will I do anything differently next meet? __

_____

Main Goal for Next Meet

_____

_____

Event & Score Goals for Next Meet

Beam _____

Bars _____

Floor _____

Vault _____

All Around _____

One Month Goals

_____

_____

_____

End of Season Goals

_____

_____

One Year Goals

_____

_____

_____

_____

My Dreams

_____

_____

_____

_____

My Thoughts

_____

_____

_____

My Scores, My Goals, My Dreams... My Journal

My Scores, My Goals, My Dreams... My Journal

Date of Meet _____

Name of Meet _____

Location of Meet _____

Level Competing Today _____

My Teammates Today _____

_____

_____

My Coach Today _____

How am I going to relax today? _____

_____

Am I ready to focus? _____

_____

Main Goal for Meet _____

_____

_____

Event & Score Goals for Today _____

Beam _____

Bars _____

Floor _____

Vault _____

All Around _____

Scores Today

Vault	Bars	Beam	Floor	AA

Did I meet my score goals? _____

What mistakes did I make today? _____

_____

Will I do anything differently next meet? _____

_____

My Scores, My Goals, My Dreams... My Journal

Main Goal for Next Meet
_____
_____

Event & Score Goals for Next Meet
Beam _____
Bars _____
Floor _____
Vault _____
All Around _____

One Month Goals
_____
_____
_____

End of Season Goals
_____
_____

One Year Goals
_____
_____
_____
_____

My Dreams
_____
_____
_____
_____

My Thoughts
_____
_____
_____

My Scores, My Goals, My Dreams... My Journal

My Scores, My Goals, My Dreams… My Journal

Date of Meet _____

Name of Meet _____

Location of Meet _____

Level Competing Today _____

My Teammates Today _____

_____

My Coach Today _____

How am I going to relax today? _____

Am I ready to focus? _____

Main Goal for Meet _____

_____

_____

Event & Score Goals for Today

Beam _____

Bars _____

Floor _____

Vault _____

All Around _____

Scores Today

Vault	Bars	Beam	Floor	AA

Did I meet my score goals? _____

What mistakes did I make today? _____

Will I do anything differently next meet? _____

_____

My Scores, My Goals, My Dreams... My Journal

Main Goal for Next Meet

_____

_____

Event & Score Goals for Next Meet

Beam _____

Bars _____

Floor _____

Vault _____

All Around _____

One Month Goals

_____

_____

_____

End of Season Goals

_____

_____

One Year Goals

_____

_____

_____

_____

My Dreams

_____

_____

_____

_____

My Thoughts

_____

_____

_____

My Scores, My Goals, My Dreams... My Journal

My Scores, My Goals, My Dreams… My Journal

My Scores, My Goals, My Dreams... My Journal

Date of Meet _____

Name of Meet _____

Location of Meet _____

Level Competing Today _____

My Teammates Today _____

_____

_____

My Coach Today _____

How am I going to relax today? _____

_____

Am I ready to focus? _____

_____

Main Goal for Meet _____

_____

_____

Event & Score Goals for Today _____

Beam _____

Bars _____

Floor _____

Vault _____

All Around _____

Scores Today

Vault	Bars	Beam	Floor	AA

Did I meet my score goals? _____

What mistakes did I make today? _____

_____

Will I do anything differently next meet? _____

_____

Main Goal for Next Meet

_____

_____

Event & Score Goals for Next Meet

Beam _____

Bars _____

Floor _____

Vault _____

All Around _____

One Month Goals

_____

_____

End of Season Goals

_____

One Year Goals

_____

_____

_____

My Dreams

_____

_____

_____

My Thoughts

_____

_____

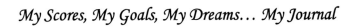
My Scores, My Goals, My Dreams… My Journal

My Scores, My Goals, My Dreams… My Journal

Date of Meet _____

Name of Meet _____

Location of Meet _____

Level Competing Today _____

My Teammates Today _____

_____

My Coach Today _____

How am I going to relax today? _____

_____

Am I ready to focus? _____

_____

Main Goal for Meet _____

_____

_____

Event & Score Goals for Today _____

Beam _____

Bars _____

Floor _____

Vault _____

All Around _____

Scores Today _____

Vault	Bars	Beam	Floor	AA

Did I meet my score goals? _____

What mistakes did I make today? _____

_____

Will I do anything differently next meet? _____

_____

Main Goal for Next Meet

_____
_____

Event & Score Goals for Next Meet

Beam _____
Bars _____
Floor _____
Vault _____
All Around _____

One Month Goals

_____
_____
_____

End of Season Goals

_____
_____

One Year Goals

_____
_____
_____
_____

My Dreams

_____
_____
_____
_____

My Thoughts

_____
_____
_____

_____
_____
_____
_____
_____
_____
_____
_____
_____
_____
_____
_____
_____
_____
_____
_____
_____
_____
_____
_____
_____
_____
_____
_____
_____
_____
_____
_____
_____
_____

My Scores, My Goals, My Dreams… My Journal

Date of Meet _____

Name of Meet _____

Location of Meet _____

Level Competing Today _____

My Teammates Today _____

_____

_____

My Coach Today _____

How am I going to relax today? _____

_____

Am I ready to focus? _____

_____

Main Goal for Meet _____

_____

_____

_____

Event & Score Goals for Today _____

Beam _____

Bars _____

Floor _____

Vault _____

All Around _____

Scores Today _____

Vault	Bars	Beam	Floor	AA

Did I meet my score goals? _____

What mistakes did I make today? _____

_____

Will I do anything differently next meet? _____

_____

Main Goal for Next Meet

_____
_____

Event & Score Goals for Next Meet

Beam _____
Bars _____
Floor _____
Vault _____
All Around _____

One Month Goals

_____
_____

End of Season Goals

_____
_____

One Year Goals

_____
_____
_____
_____

My Dreams

_____
_____
_____
_____

My Thoughts

_____
_____
_____
_____

My Scores, My Goals, My Dreams... My Journal

_____

_____

_____

_____

_____

_____

_____

_____

_____

_____

_____

_____

_____

_____

_____

_____

_____

_____

_____

_____

_____

_____

_____

_____

_____

_____

_____

_____

_____

_____

_____

My Scores, My Goals, My Dreams… My Journal

My Scores, My Goals, My Dreams... My Journal

Date of Meet _____

Name of Meet _____

Location of Meet _____

Level Competing Today _____

My Teammates Today _____

_____

My Coach Today _____

How am I going to relax today? _____

_____

Am I ready to focus? _____

_____

Main Goal for Meet _____

_____

_____

Event & Score Goals for Today _____

Beam _____

Bars _____

Floor _____

Vault _____

All Around _____

Scores Today

Vault	Bars	Beam	Floor	AA

Did I meet my score goals? _____

What mistakes did I make today? _____

_____

Will I do anything differently next meet? _____

_____

Main Goal for Next Meet

_____

_____

_____

Event & Score Goals for Next Meet

Beam _____

Bars _____

Floor _____

Vault _____

All Around _____

One Month Goals

_____

_____

_____

End of Season Goals

_____

_____

One Year Goals

_____

_____

_____

_____

My Dreams

_____

_____

_____

_____

My Thoughts

_____

_____

_____

_____
_____
_____
_____
_____
_____
_____
_____
_____
_____
_____
_____
_____
_____
_____
_____
_____
_____
_____
_____
_____
_____
_____
_____
_____
_____
_____
_____
_____
_____
_____

My Scores, My Goals, My Dreams… My Journal

Date of Meet _____

Name of Meet _____

Location of Meet _____

Level Competing Today _____

My Teammates Today _____

_____

My Coach Today _____

How am I going to relax today? _____

_____

Am I ready to focus? _____

_____

Main Goal for Meet _____

_____

_____

Event & Score Goals for Today _____

Beam _____

Bars _____

Floor _____

Vault _____

All Around _____

Scores Today

Vault	Bars	Beam	Floor	AA

Did I meet my score goals? _____

What mistakes did I make today? _____

_____

Will I do anything differently next meet? _____

_____

My Scores, My Goals, My Dreams... My Journal

Main Goal for Next Meet
_____
_____

Event & Score Goals for Next Meet
Beam _____
Bars _____
Floor _____
Vault _____
All Around _____

One Month Goals
_____
_____

End of Season Goals
_____

One Year Goals
_____
_____
_____
_____

My Dreams
_____
_____
_____
_____

My Thoughts
_____
_____
_____

_____
_____
_____
_____
_____
_____
_____
_____
_____
_____
_____
_____
_____
_____
_____
_____
_____
_____
_____
_____
_____
_____
_____
_____
_____
_____
_____
_____
_____
_____
_____
_____
_____

My Scores, My Goals, My Dreams… My Journal

Date of Meet _____
Name of Meet _____
Location of Meet _____
Level Competing Today _____
My Teammates Today _____
_____
_____
My Coach Today _____
How am I going to relax today? _____
_____
Am I ready to focus? _____
_____
Main Goal for Meet _____
_____
_____

Event & Score Goals for Today _____
Beam _____
Bars _____
Floor _____
Vault _____
All Around _____

Scores Today _____

Vault	Bars	Beam	Floor	AA

Did I meet my score goals? _____
What mistakes did I make today? _____
_____
Will I do anything differently next meet? _____
_____

Main Goal for Next Meet
_____

_____

Event & Score Goals for Next Meet

Beam _____

Bars _____

Floor _____

Vault _____

All Around _____

One Month Goals
_____

_____

End of Season Goals
_____

_____

One Year Goals
_____

_____

_____

_____

My Dreams
_____

_____

_____

My Thoughts
_____

_____

_____

My Scores, My Goals, My Dreams... My Journal

My Scores, My Goals, My Dreams… My Journal

Date of Meet _____

Name of Meet _____

Location of Meet _____

Level Competing Today _____

My Teammates Today _____

_____

_____

My Coach Today _____

How am I going to relax today? _____

_____

Am I ready to focus? _____

_____

Main Goal for Meet _____

_____

_____

Event & Score Goals for Today _____

Beam _____

Bars _____

Floor _____

Vault _____

All Around _____

Scores Today _____

Vault	Bars	Beam	Floor	AA

Did I meet my score goals? _____

What mistakes did I make today? _____

_____

Will I do anything differently next meet? __

_____

Main Goal for Next Meet

_____
_____

Event & Score Goals for Next Meet

Beam _____
Bars _____
Floor _____
Vault _____
All Around _____

One Month Goals

_____
_____

End of Season Goals

_____

One Year Goals

_____
_____
_____

My Dreams

_____
_____
_____

My Thoughts

_____
_____

My Scores, My Goals, My Dreams... My Journal

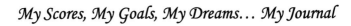

My Scores, My Goals, My Dreams… My Journal

Date of Meet _____

Name of Meet _____

Location of Meet _____

Level Competing Today _____

My Teammates Today _____

_____

My Coach Today _____

How am I going to relax today? _____

_____

Am I ready to focus? _____

_____

Main Goal for Meet _____

_____

_____

Event & Score Goals for Today _____

Beam _____

Bars _____

Floor _____

Vault _____

All Around _____

Scores Today

Vault	Bars	Beam	Floor	AA

Did I meet my score goals? _____

What mistakes did I make today? _____

_____

Will I do anything differently next meet? _____

_____

Main Goal for Next Meet

_____

_____

Event & Score Goals for Next Meet

Beam _____

Bars _____

Floor _____

Vault _____

All Around _____

One Month Goals

_____

_____

_____

End of Season Goals

_____

_____

One Year Goals

_____

_____

_____

_____

My Dreams

_____

_____

_____

_____

My Thoughts

_____

_____

_____

_____

_____

_____

_____

_____

_____

_____

_____

_____

_____

_____

_____

_____

_____

_____

_____

_____

_____

_____

_____

_____

_____

_____

_____

_____

_____

_____

_____

_____

_____

_____

_____

_____

_____

_____

My Scores, My Goals, My Dreams… My Journal

My Scores, My Goals, My Dreams… My Journal

Date of Meet _____

Name of Meet _____

Location of Meet _____

Level Competing Today _____

My Teammates Today _____

_____

_____

My Coach Today _____

How am I going to relax today? _____

_____

Am I ready to focus? _____

_____

Main Goal for Meet _____

_____

_____

Event & Score Goals for Today _____

Beam _____

Bars _____

Floor _____

Vault _____

All Around _____

Scores Today _____

Vault	Bars	Beam	Floor	AA

Did I meet my score goals? _____

What mistakes did I make today? _____

_____

Will I do anything differently next meet? _____

_____

Main Goal for Next Meet

Event & Score Goals for Next Meet

Beam

Bars

Floor

Vault

All Around

One Month Goals

End of Season Goals

One Year Goals

My Dreams

My Thoughts

_____
_____
_____
_____
_____
_____
_____
_____
_____
_____
_____
_____
_____
_____
_____
_____
_____
_____
_____
_____
_____
_____
_____
_____
_____
_____
_____
_____
_____
_____
_____

My Scores, My Goals, My Dreams… My Journal

My Scores, My Goals, My Dreams... My Journal

Date of Meet _____

Name of Meet _____

Location of Meet _____

Level Competing Today _____

My Teammates Today _____

_____

_____

My Coach Today _____

How am I going to relax today? _____

_____

Am I ready to focus? _____

_____

Main Goal for Meet _____

_____

_____

_____

Event & Score Goals for Today

Beam _____

Bars _____

Floor _____

Vault _____

All Around _____

Scores Today

Vault	Bars	Beam	Floor	AA

Did I meet my score goals? _____

What mistakes did I make today? _____

_____

Will I do anything differently next meet? _____

_____

Main Goal for Next Meet

_____

_____

Event & Score Goals for Next Meet

Beam _____

Bars _____

Floor _____

Vault _____

All Around _____

One Month Goals

_____

_____

End of Season Goals

_____

One Year Goals

_____

_____

_____

My Dreams

_____

_____

_____

My Thoughts

_____

_____

_____

My Scores, My Goals, My Dreams... My Journal

_____
_____
_____
_____
_____
_____
_____
_____
_____
_____
_____
_____
_____
_____
_____
_____
_____
_____
_____
_____
_____
_____
_____
_____
_____
_____
_____
_____
_____
_____
_____
_____
_____

My Scores, My Goals, My Dreams… My Journal

My Scores, My Goals, My Dreams... My Journal

Date of Meet _____

Name of Meet _____

Location of Meet _____

Level Competing Today _____

My Teammates Today _____

_____

_____

My Coach Today _____

How am I going to relax today? _____

_____

Am I ready to focus? _____

_____

Main Goal for Meet _____

_____

_____

_____

Event & Score Goals for Today _____

Beam _____

Bars _____

Floor _____

Vault _____

All Around _____

Scores Today

Vault	Bars	Beam	Floor	AA

Did I meet my score goals? _____

What mistakes did I make today? _____

_____

Will I do anything differently next meet? _____

_____

My Scores, My Goals, My Dreams... My Journal

Main Goal for Next Meet

Event & Score Goals for Next Meet
Beam
Bars
Floor
Vault
All Around

One Month Goals

End of Season Goals

One Year Goals

My Dreams

My Thoughts

© 2005 Goeller

My Scores, My Goals, My Dreams… My Journal

Date of Meet _____

Name of Meet _____

Location of Meet _____

Level Competing Today _____

My Teammates Today _____

_____

My Coach Today _____

How am I going to relax today? _____

Am I ready to focus? _____

Main Goal for Meet _____

_____

_____

Event & Score Goals for Today

Beam _____

Bars _____

Floor _____

Vault _____

All Around _____

Scores Today

Vault	Bars	Beam	Floor	AA

Did I meet my score goals? _____

What mistakes did I make today? _____

Will I do anything differently next meet? _____

_____

Main Goal for Next Meet

Event & Score Goals for Next Meet

Beam

Bars

Floor

Vault

All Around

One Month Goals

End of Season Goals

One Year Goals

My Dreams

My Thoughts

My Scores, My Goals, My Dreams... My Journal

_____
_____
_____
_____
_____
_____
_____
_____
_____
_____
_____
_____
_____
_____
_____
_____
_____
_____
_____
_____
_____
_____
_____
_____
_____
_____
_____
_____
_____

My Scores, My Goals, My Dreams… My Journal

Date of Meet _____

Name of Meet _____

Location of Meet _____

Level Competing Today _____

My Teammates Today _____

_____

_____

My Coach Today _____

How am I going to relax today? _____

_____

Am I ready to focus? _____

_____

Main Goal for Meet _____

_____

_____

Event & Score Goals for Today _____

Beam _____

Bars _____

Floor _____

Vault _____

All Around _____

Scores Today _____

Vault	Bars	Beam	Floor	AA

Did I meet my score goals? _____

What mistakes did I make today? _____

_____

Will I do anything differently next meet? _____

_____

Main Goal for Next Meet
_____
_____

Event & Score Goals for Next Meet
Beam _____
Bars _____
Floor _____
Vault _____
All Around _____

One Month Goals
_____
_____

End of Season Goals
_____
_____

One Year Goals
_____
_____
_____

My Dreams
_____
_____
_____

My Thoughts
_____
_____
_____

My Scores, My Goals, My Dreams... My Journal

_____
_____
_____
_____
_____
_____
_____
_____
_____
_____
_____
_____
_____
_____
_____
_____
_____
_____
_____
_____
_____
_____
_____
_____
_____
_____
_____
_____
_____
_____
_____
_____
_____
_____

My Scores, My Goals, My Dreams… My Journal

Date of Meet _____

Name of Meet _____

Location of Meet _____

Level Competing Today _____

My Teammates Today _____

_____

My Coach Today _____

How am I going to relax today? _____

_____

Am I ready to focus? _____

_____

Main Goal for Meet _____

_____

_____

Event & Score Goals for Today _____

Beam _____

Bars _____

Floor _____

Vault _____

All Around _____

Scores Today

Vault	Bars	Beam	Floor	AA

Did I meet my score goals? _____

What mistakes did I make today? _____

_____

Will I do anything differently next meet? ___

_____

Main Goal for Next Meet

_____

_____

Event & Score Goals for Next Meet

Beam _____

Bars _____

Floor _____

Vault _____

All Around _____

One Month Goals

_____

_____

End of Season Goals

_____

One Year Goals

_____

_____

_____

My Dreams

_____

_____

_____

My Thoughts

_____

_____

_____

My Scores, My Goals, My Dreams... My Journal

<u>Date of Meet</u>

<u>Name of Meet</u>

<u>Location of Meet</u>

<u>Level Competing Today</u>

<u>My Teammates Today</u>

<u>My Coach Today</u>

<u>How am I going to relax today?</u>

<u>Am I ready to focus?</u>

<u>Main Goal for Meet</u>

<u>Event & Score Goals for Today</u>

<u>Beam</u>

<u>Bars</u>

<u>Floor</u>

<u>Vault</u>

<u>All Around</u>

<u>Scores Today</u>

<u>Vault</u>	Bars	Beam	Floor	AA

<u>Did I meet my score goals?</u>

<u>What mistakes did I make today?</u>

<u>Will I do anything differently next meet?</u>

© 2005 Goeller

Main Goal for Next Meet _____

_____

_____

Event & Score Goals for Next Meet _____

Beam _____

Bars _____

Floor _____

Vault _____

All Around _____

One Month Goals _____

_____

_____

_____

End of Season Goals _____

_____

_____

One Year Goals _____

_____

_____

_____

_____

My Dreams _____

_____

_____

_____

_____

My Thoughts _____

_____

_____

_____

My Scores, My Goals, My Dreams... My Journal

My Scores, My Goals, My Dreams… My Journal

My Scores, My Goals, My Dreams... My Journal

Date of Meet _____

Name of Meet _____

Location of Meet _____

Level Competing Today _____

My Teammates Today _____

_____

_____

My Coach Today _____

How am I going to relax today? _____

_____

Am I ready to focus? _____

_____

Main Goal for Meet _____

_____

_____

_____

Event & Score Goals for Today _____

Beam _____

Bars _____

Floor _____

Vault _____

All Around _____

Scores Today

Vault	Bars	Beam	Floor	AA

Did I meet my score goals? _____

What mistakes did I make today? _____

_____

Will I do anything differently next meet? __

_____

Main Goal for Next Meet

_____
_____

Event & Score Goals for Next Meet

Beam _____
Bars _____
Floor _____
Vault _____
All Around _____

One Month Goals

_____
_____
_____

End of Season Goals

_____
_____

One Year Goals

_____
_____
_____
_____

My Dreams

_____
_____
_____
_____

My Thoughts

_____
_____
_____

My Scores, My Goals, My Dreams... My Journal

My Scores, My Goals, My Dreams… My Journal

My Scores, My Goals, My Dreams… My Journal

Date of Meet _____

Name of Meet _____

Location of Meet _____

Level Competing Today _____

My Teammates Today _____

_____

_____

My Coach Today _____

How am I going to relax today? _____

_____

Am I ready to focus? _____

_____

Main Goal for Meet _____

_____

_____

Event & Score Goals for Today _____

Beam _____

Bars _____

Floor _____

Vault _____

All Around _____

Scores Today

Vault	Bars	Beam	Floor	AA

Did I meet my score goals? _____

What mistakes did I make today? _____

_____

Will I do anything differently next meet? _____

_____

Main Goal for Next Meet

_____

_____

Event & Score Goals for Next Meet

Beam _____

Bars _____

Floor _____

Vault _____

All Around _____

One Month Goals

_____

_____

End of Season Goals

_____

_____

One Year Goals

_____

_____

_____

_____

My Dreams

_____

_____

_____

_____

My Thoughts

_____

_____

_____

My Scores, My Goals, My Dreams… My Journal

My Scores, My Goals, My Dreams... My Journal

Date of Meet _____

Name of Meet _____

Location of Meet _____

Level Competing Today _____

My Teammates Today _____

_____

My Coach Today _____

How am I going to relax today? _____

_____

Am I ready to focus? _____

_____

Main Goal for Meet _____

_____

_____

Event & Score Goals for Today _____

Beam _____

Bars _____

Floor _____

Vault _____

All Around _____

Scores Today

Vault	Bars	Beam	Floor	AA

Did I meet my score goals? _____

What mistakes did I make today? _____

_____

Will I do anything differently next meet? _____

_____

Main Goal for Next Meet

_____
_____

Event & Score Goals for Next Meet

Beam _____
Bars _____
Floor _____
Vault _____
All Around _____

One Month Goals

_____
_____
_____

End of Season Goals

_____
_____

One Year Goals

_____
_____
_____
_____

My Dreams

_____
_____
_____
_____

My Thoughts

_____
_____
_____

My Scores, My Goals, My Dreams... My Journal

_____
_____
_____
_____
_____
_____
_____
_____
_____
_____
_____
_____
_____
_____
_____
_____
_____
_____
_____
_____
_____
_____
_____
_____
_____
_____
_____
_____
_____
_____
_____

My Scores, My Goals, My Dreams… My Journal

Other books by this author…

Gymnastics Drills and Conditioning Exercises
ISBN # 1-4116-0579-9

Gymnastics Drills and Conditioning for the Walkover, Limber, and Back Handspring
ISBN # 1-4116-1160-8

Gymnastics Conditioning for the Legs and Ankles
ISBN # 1-4116-2033-X

Gymnastics Drills and Conditioning for the Handstand
ISBN # 1-4116-5000-X

The Most Frequently Asked Questions About Gymnastics
ISBN # 1-59113-372-6

Over 100 Drills and Conditioning Exercises
ISBN # 1-4116-0296-X This is an earlier version of 1-4116-0579-9.

For more information on drills and conditioning books visit
www.GymnasticsDrills.com.
For gymnastics equipment, apparel, supplies, and gifts visit
www.GymnasticsStuff.com.

My Scores, My Goals, My Dreams… My Journal

LaVergne, TN USA
27 August 2010
194944LV00001B/32/A